Instant Pot

5 Ingredients or Less.

Easy, Delicious & Healthy Instant Pot Recipes for Your Family

Sandy N. Jones

Table of Contents

•Pork & Fish

•Beef

Introduction:

The Instant Pot is an amazing appliance that is going to be able to cook all of your favorite meals in record time, most of the recipes not taking more than 20 minutes to complete.

The sauté option on the Instant Pot also allows you to cook all of your dishes without dirtying another pot, pan, or skillet. It also sautes more uniformly than on the stove top and since it has a non-stick surface, nothing gets caked on the bottom of the pot.

Unlike other pressure cookers, the Instant Pot allows you to switch from one cooking option to another! This means that if you have to sauté your meat, you can do it right in the Instant Pot, then switch over to the pressure cooking option or the slow cooker option.

The Instant Pot is very easy to use as well. While it might seem that all of the buttons and beeps would be a bit confusing, as long as you read the manual that comes with the Instant Pot, you will easily be able to understand how it works. It is very important that you read the manual, we must not forget that this is still a pressure cooker and it can be dangerous if you use it without being informed as to how it works.

While it is quite obvious that the Instant Pot can do anything that any other pressure cooker can do, what most people love about the Instant Pot is that it can do it all, not just pressure cook. You can steam a cake, make cheesecake, cook your oats, cook food from the frozen state in no time flat, make pasta, rice and on and on.

Cleaning the Instant Pot is easy as well. You can pop the inner pot into the dishwasher if you desire, but all it really needs is a quick soapy wipe down after use because of the non-stick surface, nothing sticks making it very easy to clean.

The Instant Pot is the perfect appliance for anyone who lives a busy lifestyle or one that is always on the go. Stay at home moms, bloggers, and busy businesswomen have raved about how much they love their Instant Pot and how much easier it has made their life.

One of the greatest benefits that many people find besides the fact that they can cook their meals in no time flat, is that if they forget to lay something out for dinner, they do not have to worry because they can cook the food from the frozen state in under 20 minutes.

There is no other appliance out there that does all that the Instant Pot can do and there is no other appliance that can save you as much time as the Instant Pot can.

Throughout the rest of this book, we are going to be going over many Instant Pot recipes that are five ingredients or less.

The book is broken down by meal and to ensure that you are able to find just what you are looking for, you will find that each chapter is broken down into sections.

If you are new to the Instant Pot or if you have been using it for some time now, you are going to find plenty of delicious, easy recipes in this book that all take only five ingredients or less.

Chapter 1- Instant Pot Breakfasts Five Ingredients or Less

Breakfast really is the most important meal of the day. It allows us to break the fast that we have been on while we were sleeping and when you eat a healthy breakfast, it will help to boost your metabolism. Sadly, few people are actually taking the time to eat a healthy breakfast and while eating that fast food breakfast sandwich that you purchased at the drive-thru is better than not eating anything at all, now that you have the Instant Pot, there really is no excuse for you not to be preparing healthy homemade breakfasts, in an INSTANT!

This chapter is divided into two sections, the first section is breakfast recipes that contain eggs. The second section is comprised of breakfast recipes that are based on hot cereal such a quinoa or steel cut oats. No matter what it is that you are in the mood for this morning, you are sure to find something in this chapter that you will love.

Eggs:

1. Breakfast Pie

Serves 4. Prep Time: 10 Mins, Cook Time: 8 Mins

You will need:

8 eggs

1 sweet potato

1 pound of sausage, broken up

1 yellow onion

1 tbsp. of garlic powder.

You can also use salt and pepper to taste or other vegetables such as peppers.

Instructions:

1. Begin by spraying the inside of the Instant Pot with nonstick cooking spray. Shred the sweet potato and whisk the eggs until all of the yolks are broken.

2. Place all of the ingredients into the Instant Pot and cook for 8 minutes on high pressure.

3. After the Instant Pot has beeped, signaling that the cooking process has completed, use the quick release option and slice like a pie. Serve hot.

2. Cheesy Egg Bake

Serves 4. Prep Time: 10 Minutes, Cook Time: 7 Minutes

You will need:

8 eggs

1/2 of a cup of milk

1 cup of sharp cheddar cheese, shredded

5 slices of bacon, cooked crispy and diced (or 1 cup of diced ham)

2 cups of hash brown potatoes, make sure that these are thawed and not frozen

You may also choose to add some salt or use green onions as a garnish.

Instructions:

1. Place the bacon in the bottom of the Instant Pot. Next, make a layer of with the hash brown potatoes, then sprinkle 1/2 of a cup of cheddar cheese on top of the hash brown potatoes.

2. In a separate bowl, you will want to whisk the eggs and milk together, then pour that mixture over the hash brown potatoes.

3. Sprinkle the remaining cheddar cheese over the top.

4. Place the lid on the Instant Pot and ensure that it is locked into place. Make sure that the valve is closed as well.

5. Using high pressure, cook for 7 minutes.

6. After the Instant Pot beeps, you will want to go ahead and use the quick pressure release, even though there should be no pressure. Serve hot.

3. Ham, Egg, and Cheese casserole

Serves 5 - 6. Prep Time: 5 Minutes, Cook Time: 7 Hours

You will need:

32 ounces back of frozen hash browns, cubed

2 cups of ham, diced

2 cups of sharp cheddar, shredded

12 eggs

1 cup of milk

You can also choose to add in onions, peppers or other vegetables as well as season with salt and pepper.

Instructions:

1. Begin by spraying the inside of the Instant Pot with nonstick cooking spray. Put about a third of the hash browns on the bottom of the Instant Pot. Next place 1/3 of the ham, and then 1/3 of the cheese.
2. Repeat this layering 2 more times, until you run out of ingredients.
3. In a separate bowl, you will mix the eggs and the milk and whisk them until they are mixed well. Pour this over the layers in the Instant Pot.
4. Choose the slow cooker option and then adjust the time to 7 hours. This is a great breakfast to make while you are sleeping and wake up to the next morning.

4. Poached Eggs

Serves 4. Prep Time: 5 Minutes, Cook Time: 2 Minutes

You will need:

4 eggs

1 cup of water

4 silicone baking cups

Instructions:

1. Begin by cracking each egg into a silicone baking cup. Place the trivet into the bottom of the Instant Pot and place the silicone baking cups on top of it.

2. Pour the 1 cup of water into the Instant Pot so that it is under the eggs.

3. Place the lid on the Instant Pot and ensure that it is locked into place. Using the steam setting cook the eggs for 2 minutes, then allow the pressure to naturally release for an additional 3 minutes.

4. After the pressure has released, lift the lid and take the eggs out of the Instant Pot. Pour them out of the baking cups onto plates.

5. Serve with salt and pepper.

5. Steamed Eggs (Korean Style)

Serves 1. Prep Time: 5 Minutes, Cook Time: 5 Minutes

You will need:

1 egg

1/3 of a cup of tap water

Scallions, chopped

Sesame seeds, no more than a pinch

Garlic powder, salt, and pepper to taste

Instructions:

1. Begin by cracking the egg into a bowl filled with 1/3 of a cup of tap water and mix well. Next, you will want to strain the egg and water, using a fine mesh strainer and into a bowl that is heat proof.

2. Next, you will mix in the rest of the ingredients and stir well. Place 1 cup of water into the Instant Pot, followed by the steamer basket or the trivet. Place the bowl with the mixture in it on the steamer or trivet.

3. Lock the lid in place. Cook on high pressure for 5 minutes. When the Instant Pot beeps, signaling that the egg is done cooking, do a quick release and serve.

4. This is great with rice.

Hot Cereals

1. Breakfast Quinoa

Serves 1. Prep Time: 5 Minutes, Cook Time: 1 Minute

You will need:

1 1/2 cups of quinoa, uncooked and rinsed well

2 1/4 cups of water

2 tbsp. Maple syrup

1/2 of a tsp. of vanilla

1/4 of a teaspoon cinnamon, ground

Optional: You can top this with berries, almonds, or milk.

Instructions:

1. Place the water, quinoa, cinnamon, syrup and vanilla into the Instant Pot. Lock the lid in place and then cook for 1 minute on the high-pressure setting. After the Instant Pot beeps, signaling that the cooking stage is done, allow the quinoa to sit for 10 minutes then use the quick pressure release in order to ensure all of the pressure has been released.

2. Remove the lid and fluff with a fork. Serve hot with optional toppings.

2. Bacon, Egg and Cheese Biscuit Casserole

Serves 4. Prep Time: 5 Minutes, Cook Time: 5 Minutes

You will need:

1 pack of bacon cooked crispy and chopped into small pieces

1 dozen eggs

One 8 ounce pack of sharp cheddar cheese

1 pack of biscuit dough

Instructions:

1. Begin by opening up the roll of biscuit dough and tearing the biscuits into 8 pieces each. Place the Pieces into the Instant Pot.

2. In a separate bowl, you will crack all of the eggs and mix them well ensuring that all of the yolks are broken. Add in the bacon pieces and mix.

3. Pour the mixture over the biscuits. Close the Instant Pot lid and lock it into place. Cook on high pressure for 5 minutes.

4. After the Instant Pot beeps signaling that the food is done cooking, you will do a quick release and scoop the mixture out onto plates to be served. Sprinkle with cheddar cheese.

3. Oats in A Jar

Serves 1. Prep Time: 5 Minutes, Cook Time: 12 Minutes

You will need:

1 cup of steel cut oats

1 cup of almond milk

1 cup of vanilla Greek yogurt

3 tablespoons of chia seeds

1 cup of fresh blueberries

3 small mason jars

Instructions:

1. Begin by placing 1/3 of a cup of steel cut oats, 1/3 of a cup of almond milk, 1/3 of a cup of vanilla Greek yogurt, 1 tablespoon of chia seeds and 1/3 of a cup of fresh blueberries into each mason jar.
2. Cover each jar with a piece of foil to ensure that water does not go into the jar. Add the trivet into the Instant Pot.
3. Place 1 1/2 of a cup of water into the Instant Pot and then place your jars onto the trivet. Place the lid on the Instant Pot and make sure that it locks into place.
4. Using the rice setting you will cook your oats for 12 minutes. After the Instant Pot beeps indicating that the cooking process is complete, use the quick pressure release.
5. Remove the jars from the Instant Pot and serve hot.

4. Instant Quinoa

Serves 1. Prep Time: 5 Minutes, Cook Time: 4 Minutes

You will need:

1 cup of quinoa

2 cups of water

Dried fruit, nuts, seeds or maple syrup for topping.

Instructions:

1. Place the quinoa and the 2 cups of water into the Instant Pot along with whatever extra topping you choose.

2. Close the lid and lock it into place. Cook for 4 minutes on high pressure. After the quinoa has cooked, do a quick release and remove the lid. Stir the quinoa ensuring that everything is mixed well and serve hot.

5. Hot Cocoa Steel Cut Oats

Serves 4. Prep Time: 5 Minutes, Cook Time: 12 Minutes

You will need:

1 cup of steel cut oats

3 cups of water

1/3 of a cup of brown sugar

1/3 of a cup of hot cocoa mix

Instructions:

1. Begin by spraying the Instant Pot with nonstick cooking spray to ensure that the steel cut oats do not stick to the sides.

2. Next, you will mix all of the ingredients in a large bowl and then pour them into the Instant Pot. Cook using the rice setting for 12 minutes.

3. After the Instant Pot beeps, signaling that the cooking cycle has been completed, you will do a quick release and serve the oats hot.

6. Apple Oats

Serves 2. Prep Time: 5 Minutes, Cook Time: 4 Minutes

You will need:

1 Cup. of steel cut oats

1/2 of a cup of plain Greek yogurt

1.5 cups of water

2 apples, cored and chopped, peel on

1/2 of a cup of maple syrup

You can also include cinnamon, cloves, and slivered almonds if you want

Instructions:

1. Begin by placing everything into the Instant Pot. Cover and make sure that the lid has locked into place and that the valve is sealed.

2. Cook on high for 4 minutes. After the oats have cooked, you will do a quick release, stir well and serve hot.

Chapter 2- Instant Pot Lunches Five Ingredients or Less

Not only is the Instant Pot great for making quick breakfasts but it can also help you to make some healthy fast lunches for those days when the entire family is home! This chapter is going to be broken down into several sections, allowing you to find the exact type of recipe that you are looking for, and of course, each of the recipes in this chapter are going to use only five ingredients or less. This chapter is going to include recipes in several different sections, including soups, rice, chicken, beef, and pork.

Soups

1. Potato Soup

Serves 5. Prep Time: 10 Minutes, Cook Time: 20 Minutes

You will need:

5 pounds of golden potatoes

1/2 of a cup of cheddar cheese

1 cup of bacon, chopped

1 bundle of green onions

2 cups chicken broth

2 cups water

Instructions:

1. If you want to peel your potatoes, you will want to do this first, however, it is not necessary. If you want to get the extra nutrients from the potato peel, simply leave it on the potato.

2. Next, you will dice the potatoes into about 1/2 inch pieces, the smaller you can dice them the better. Place all of the potatoes as well as the chicken broth and water into the Instant Pot. Lock the lid into place and cook on high pressure for 20 minutes.

3. After the potatoes have cooked for 20 minutes, you will use the quick pressure release option and remove the potatoes from the instant pot placing them in a

bowl with 3/4 of a cup of bacon bits. Mash the potatoes using a hand mixer or immersion blender. As you are mixing the potatoes, you will slowly add in the liquid from the Instant Pot.

4. Serve topped with the remainder of the bacon, green onions and a bit of cheddar cheese.

2. Bean Soup

Serves 4. Prep Time: 10 Minutes, Cook Time: 40 Minutes

You will need:

A bag of 15 bean soup mix

2 teaspoons of chili powder

1 can, diced tomatoes

1/2 of an onion chopped and 1 teaspoon of garlic

1 ham hock

8 cups of water

Instructions:

1. The first thing that you want to do is wash your beans. You can place them in a pasta strainer in order to rinse them off but you need to make sure they are clean. You should also pick through them to ensure there are no rocks.

2. Next, you will place the beans in the Instant Pot, add in the 8 cups of water, the onion as well as the ham hock.

3. Place the lid on your Instant Pot and lock it into place. Cook using the bean mode. After the beans are cooked, you will use the quick release option and add in the tomatoes, chili powder as well as the seasoning pack that came in the 15 bean soup mix. Stir.

4. Place the lid back onto the Instant Pot and cook for 10 more minutes using the bean setting. After the beans have cooked, allow the pressure to naturally release for 10 minutes. Serve the soup hot.

3. Taco Soup

Serves 4. Prep Time: 10 Minutes, Cook Time: 10 Minutes

You will Need:

1 pound ground beef

1 pack taco seasoning

1 can black beans, rinsed and drained

1 can kidney beans, rinsed and drained

1 can of diced tomatoes with green chilies

Instructions:

Begin by breaking up the ground beef in the Instant Pot and brown using the sauté mode. Make sure that you stir the ground beef while it is cooking in order to ensure that it does not stick or burn. After the beef has browned you will want to drain off any excess fat.

Place all of the ingredients into the Instant Pot as well as enough water to cover everything. Lock the lid into place and cook on high pressure for about 10 minutes. After the Instant Pot beeps, signaling that the taco soup is done, you will do a quick release and serve the soup hot.

This soup is great served with sour cream, cheese or tortilla chips.

Rice

1. Broccoli and Cheese Rice

Serves 2. Prep Time: 10 Minutes, Cook Time: 15 Minutes

You will need:

4 ounces of cream cheese, softened and cut into pieces

1 cup of shredded sharp cheddar

1/2 of a cup of chopped onion

1 cup of white or brown rice

3 cups of fresh broccoli, chopped

2 1/2 cups of water

Instructions:

1. This is a very easy recipe. All you have to do is place all of the ingredients into the instant pot, except for the cheddar cheese. Lock the lid into place and cook on high pressure for 15 minutes. After the rice has cooked, use the quick release option and mix in the cheddar cheese. It should melt quickly. Serve hot

2. If you are concerned that the rice is going to stick to the sides of your Instant Pot, simply spray the inside of the Instant Pot with cooking spray.

2. Pineapple Rice

Serves 2. Prep Time: 10 Minutes, Cook Time: 7 Minutes

You will need:

1 cup of white rice

1 cup of water

1/4 of a cup of pineapple juice (this can be the juice that comes out of the can of crushed pineapple)

8 ounces of crushed pineapple, (use this juice)

1 tablespoon of butter

Instructions:

Place all of the ingredients into the Instant Pot. Place the lid on and lock it into place. Cook the rice on the high pressure for 7 minutes. After the rice has cooked, allow the pressure to naturally release for 2 minutes.

Serve hot.

Chicken

1. Buffalo Ranch Chicken

Serves 4. Prep Time: 10 Minutes, Cook Time: 20 Minutes

You will need:

4 chicken breasts, boneless and skinless, thawed

One 12 ounce bottle of Franks RedHot Buffalo Sauce

1 packet of ranch seasoning mix

Instructions:

1. Begin by placing the chicken in the Instant Pot. In a bowl, mix the Buffalo sauce and the ranch seasoning mix together and pour over the chicken. Lock the lid into place and cook for 20 minutes on high pressure.

2. After the chicken has cooked, use the quick pressure release method and remove the chicken from the Instant Pot, placing it on a plate. Shred it with two forks and placed back into the Instant Pot coating it with the liquid.

3. Place on a bun for a great sandwich! Serve hot.

2. TSO Chili Chicken

Serves 4. Prep Time: 15 Minutes, Cook Time: 20 - 30 Minutes

You will need:

4 chicken breasts, boneless and skinless, thawed

1 bottle or 12.6 ounces of TSAO sauce

8 Thai Chilies, dried

2 green onions, chopped

Sesame seeds

Instructions:

1. Place the chicken, TSAO sauce, and Thai Chilies into the Instant pot. Lock the lid in place and cook for 20 minutes. After the Instant Pot beeps, signaling that the chicken is done, you will do a quick pressure release and remove the chicken from the Instant Pot.

2. Cut the chicken into cubes. If you see any pink, place the chicken back into the Instant Pot and cook for another 10 minutes. (timing will depend on how large the chicken breasts are, in general, you should cook the chicken for 10 minutes per pound)

3. After the chicken is done cooking you will remove it from the Instant Pot and serve over rice garnished with sesame seeds and green onions.

3. Bacon Ranch BBQ Chicken

Serves 4. Prep Time: 15 Minutes, Cook Time: 20 Minutes

You will need:

4 chicken breasts, boneless and skinless, thawed

1 bottle of your favorite BBQ sauce

1 packet of ranch seasoning mix

1 pack of bacon, that has been cooked and chopped

Instructions:

1. Place the chicken breasts in the Instant Pot. In a separate bowl, mix the BBQ sauce and the Ranch seasoning packet as well as the bacon. Pour this mixture over the chicken.

2. Lock the lid in place and using the poultry setting cook for 20 minutes. Serve hot.

4. Alfredo Chicken with Bacon

Serves 4. Prep Time: 15 Minutes, Cook Time: 20 Minutes

You will need:

> 4 chicken breasts, boneless and skinless, thawed
>
> 6 slices of hickory bacon, cooked crispy and chopped
>
> 1 jar of your favorite alfredo sauce, about 15 ounces
>
> 1 cup of shredded Mozzarella
>
> 4 ounces of mushroom pieces, drained

Instructions:

1. Begin by placing the chicken breast in the instant pot. Pour the alfredo sauce over the chicken, then add the mushroom pieces and top with the bacon. Close the lid and lock it into place. Cook on the poultry setting for 20 minutes.

2. Use the quick release option and then sprinkle with the mozzarella cheese. The cheese should melt quickly. This can be served as a main course or with pasta.

5. Pepperoni Chicken

Serves 4. Prep Time: 15 Minutes, Cook Time: 20 Minutes

You will need:

4 chicken breasts, boneless and skinless, thawed

One 14 ounce jar of your favorite pizza sauce

1 cup of shredded mozzarella

16 pepperoni slices

Instructions:

1. Begin by placing the chicken breasts in the instant pot. Then pour the pizza sauce over the chicken breasts and top the breasts with the pepperoni.

2. Lock the lid into place and cook on the poultry setting for 20 minutes. After the chicken has cooked, you will use the quick release option and then sprinkle the mozzarella cheese over the chicken. Allow the cheese to melt and then serve hot.

6. Orange Chicken

Serves 4. Prep Time: 15 Minutes, Cook Time: 20 Minutes

You will need:

4 chicken breasts, boneless and skinless, thawed

3/4 of a cup of orange marmalade

3/4 of a cup of your favorite BBQ sauce

2 tablespoons of soy sauce

Instructions:

1. Begin by placing the chicken in the Instant Pot. Next, you will want to mix the marmalade, BBQ sauce, and the soy sauce in a small bowl and pour it over the chicken.

2. Lock the lid into place and cook using the poultry setting for 20 minutes. After the Instant Pot beeps indicating that the chicken is completely cooked, you will use the quick release option and serve the chicken hot. This is great served over rice.

7. Simple Italian Chicken

Serves 4. Prep Time: 10 Minutes, Cook Time: 20 Minutes

You will need:

4 chicken breasts, boneless and skinless, thawed

1 bottle of Italian dressing, about 16 ounces

Instructions:

1. Begin by placing the chicken breasts in the bottom of the Instant Pot. Next, you will pour the dressing over the chicken breasts. Close the lid and lock it into place. Cook using the poultry setting for 20 minutes.

2. When the Instant Pot beeps signaling that the chicken is completely cooked, you will use the quick release option and serve the chicken hot.

8. Lemon Pepper and Garlic Chicken

Serves 4. Prep Time: 15 Minutes, Cook Time: 20 Minutes

You will need:

> 4 chicken breasts, boneless and skinless, thawed
>
> 1 can of cream of chicken soup with herbs
>
> 1 can of cream of mushroom soup with garlic
>
> 4 garlic cloves, minced
>
> The juice from 1 lemon

Instructions:

1. Begin by placing the chicken breasts in the Instant Pot. In a separate bowl, you will want to mix the cream of chicken, cream of mushroom, minced garlic and lemon juice.

2. P our the soup mixture over the chicken breasts. Close the lid and ensure that it is locked into place. Using the poultry setting cook the chicken for 20 minutes. After the chicken has cooked, use the quick release option and serve hot. This is great with a side of rice.

9. Whole Chicken (Ranch Onion)

Serves 4. Prep Time: 15 Minutes, Cook Time: 50 Minutes

You will need:

1 whole chicken that is about 4 to 5 pounds

1 onion soup mix packet

1 ranch mix packet

3 cloves of garlic, peeled and crushed

1 teaspoon of paprika

Instructions:

Begin by placing all of the dry ingredients into a small bowl and mixing them well to create a rub for the chicken. Next, you will want to rinse the chicken off and remove all of the innards. Pat the chicken dry with a paper towel.

Next, you are going to place the three crushed garlic cloves inside the chicken. Place the chicken into your Instant Pot. Choose the poultry option then add an extra 20-30 minutes for a 4-5 pound chicken (10 minutes per pound of chicken for the total cooking time).

After the Instant Pot beeps indicating that the chicken is done, do a quick release and check to ensure that here is no pink left. If there is still pink in the chicken, cook for an additional 10 minutes. When the chicken is done cooking remove from the Instant Pot and serve hot.

Beef

1. Broccoli and Beef

Serves 4. Prep Time: 15 Minutes, Cook Time: 20 Minutes

You will need:

1 1/2 pounds of flank steak that has been trimmed of the fat

One 14 ounce bag of frozen broccoli

One 8 ounce packet of broccoli beef sauce

1/4 of a cup of water

Instructions:

Begin by cutting the flank steak against the grain into strips that are about ½ of an inch thick. After you have cut the steak into strips, you will want to cut the strips into shorter pieces that are about 2 inches long.

Place the steak into the Instant Pot and pour the 1/4 of a cup of water over the steak. Next, pour the broccoli beef sauce over the steak and close the lid on the Instant Pot. Lock the lid into place and cook for 20 minutes on high pressure.

While the beef is cooking, you will place your broccoli into a microwave safe bowl and warm it for 1 minute at a time until it is thawed.

After the Instant Pot beeps, indicating that the beef is done cooking, you will use a quick release and open the pot. Switch over to the sauté mode and mix the broccoli into the beef mixture. Stir well until the sauce begins to thicken.

Turn the Instant Pot off and serve hot. This is great over rice.

2. Beef Fajitas

Serves 4. Prep Time: 15 Minutes, Cook Time: 30 - 45 Minutes

You will need:

A 3-pound roast (chuck is suggested)

1 can of fire roasted tomatoes, diced, about 15 ounces

1 can of corn, drained, about 15 ounces

1 can of red kidney beans, rinsed and drained

2 chipotles in adobo sauce, roughly chopped

For the fajitas, you will need tortillas and optional toppings include sour cream, Mexican blend cheese or cilantro.

Instructions:

Begin by seasoning the roast with salt and pepper if desired and placing it into the Instant Pot (if you want the roast to cook faster you can cut it into smaller bits)

Next, you will add in the diced tomatoes, corn, red kidney beans and chopped chipotles. Close the lid and ensure that it is locked into place. Cook on high pressure for about 30 minutes. After the Instant Pot beeps signaling that the roast has cooked, do a quick release and using a fork check to see if the roast is tender enough. If not, continue to cook for about 15 more minutes on high pressure.

After the roast has cooked, remove it from the Instant Pot and place it on a plate. Using two forks, shred the roast. Scoop out the corn mixture that is in the Instant Pot and mix it with the shredded beef.

Serve on tortillas.

3. BBQ Ranch Meatballs

Serves 4. Prep Time: 10 Minutes, Cook Time: 4 Minutes

You will need:

26 ounces of frozen meatballs

One 18 ounce bottle of your favorite BBQ sauce

1 packet of ranch dressing mix

Instructions:

In a bowl, mix the BBQ sauce and the ranch dressing mix. Place the frozen meatballs into the Instant Pot and pour the BBQ sauce mixture over them.

Close the lid and ensure that it is locked into place. Cook using the high-pressure setting for 4 minutes. Do a quick steam release and serve hot.

4. Buffalo Ranch Meatballs

Serves 4. Prep Time: 10 Minutes, Cook Time: 4 Minutes

You will need:

1 bag of Italian Style frozen meatballs, about 26 ounces

One 12 ounce bottle of Frank's Red Hot Wings Buffalo sauce

1 packet of dry ranch dressing mix

Instructions:

Mix the buffalo sauce and the ranch dressing mix in a small bowl. Place the frozen meatballs into the Instant Pot and pour the buffalo sauce mixture over the top of them. Close the lid and lock it into place. Cook on high pressure for 4 minutes.

After the Instant Pot beeps, indicating that the cooking process is done, you will do a quick release and serve the meatballs hot.

5. Sweet and Sour Meatballs

Serves 4. Prep Time: 10 Minutes, Cook Time: 4 Minutes

You will need:

One 26 ounce bag of frozen meatballs

One 12 ounce bottle of sweet and sour sauce

Sesame seeds

Instructions:

Begin by placing the frozen meatballs into the Instant pot and pouring the sweet and sour sauce over them. Close the lid and ensure that it is locked into place. Cook on high pressure for 4 minutes.

After the Instant Pot beeps indicating that the cooking process is complete, you will do a quick release and sprinkle the sesame seeds over the meatballs. Serve hot. This is great served over rice.

6. Italian Beef For Sandwiches

Serves 4. Prep Time: 15 Minutes, Cook Time: 45 Minutes

You will need:

> 3 pound chuck roast, fat trimmed and cut into chunks
>
> 1 pack of Italian salad dressing mix
>
> One 8 ounce jar of pepperoncini sliced peppers as well as a splash of the juice from the jar
>
> One 8 ounce Giardiniera sandwich mix drained
>
> One 14.5 ounce can of beef broth
>
> In order to make the sandwiches, you will need provolone cheese and hoagie buns

Instructions:

> Begin by placing the roast in the bottom of the Instant Pot. Sprinkle the Italian salad dressing mix over the roast and then add the pepperoncini peppers as well as the beef broth, a splash of the pepper juice and the giardiniera.
>
> Place the lid on the Instant Pot and ensure that it is locked into place. Cook on high pressure for 45 minutes.
>
> After the Instant Pot beeps, signaling that the roast has completed the cooking process, do a quick release and shred the beef.

In order to make sandwiches, you will scoop the meat mixture onto hoagie buns and top with provolone cheese.

7. Steak Pizzaiola

Serves 4. Prep Time: 15 Minutes, Cook Time: 45 - 60 Minutes

You will need:

1 - 2 pound London broil

1 medium onion, sliced

1 bell pepper, color of your choice, seeded and sliced

12 ounces of pasta sauce

1/4 of a cup of water

Instructions:

Begin by placing the London broil in the instant pot. (if you want this to cook faster you can cut it into chunks)

Cover the broil with the sliced onions, bell pepper, pasta sauce, and water. Place the lid on the Instant Pot and lock it into place.

Using the high setting, cook this for 45 minutes. After the Instant Pot has beeped, indicating that the cooking process is over, you will do a quick release and then check to ensure that the meat is tender. If you want it to be more tender, continue to cook for another 15 minutes.

After the broil has finished cooking you will remove it from the Instant Pot along with the vegetables and serve hot.

This is great served over pasta, potatoes or with bread.

8. Sweet and Spicy Meatballs

Serves 4. Prep Time: 15 Minutes, Cook Time: 4 Minutes

You will need:

2 pounds of frozen meatballs

One 16 ounce jar of apple cinnamon salsa

2 cups of dried cranberries

1 1/2 cups of apple juice

Instructions:

Begin by placing the meatballs into the Instant Pot. Cover the meatballs with the rest of the ingredients. Place the lid on the Instant Pot and lock it into place. Cook on high pressure for 4 minutes.

After the Instant Pot beeps indicating that the meatballs are done cooking, you will do a quick release and serve the meatballs hot.

These are great served over rice.

Pork

1. White Beans and Sausage

Serves 4. Prep Time: 15 Minutes, Cook Time: 30 Minutes

You will need:

> 4 cups of white beans
>
> 1 jar of crushed tomatoes, 25 ounces
>
> 1 tbsp. of garlic powder
>
> 1 tbsp. of salt
>
> 12 ounces of kielbasa sausage

Instructions:

> Begin by washing your beans and picking through them. Place the beans in the Instant Pot and cover them with water. Stir in the garlic powder, tomatoes, and salt. Cut the sausage into bite-sized pieces and add it to the Instant Pot.
>
> Cook on high for 30 minutes. After the Instant Pot beeps signaling that the beans are done cooking, you will want to allow the pressure to release naturally and serve hot. You can add more salt or garlic after they have finished cooking if you would like.

2. Smokey Baby Back Ribs

Serves 4. Prep Time: 15 Minutes, Cook Time: 30 Minutes

You will need:

2.5 pounds of baby back pork ribs

1/2 of a teaspoon of smoked paprika

For the glaze, you will need:

1.5 tablespoons of your favorite BBQ sauce

1.5 tablespoons of hoisin sauce

Instructions:

Begin by spraying the inside of the Instant Pot with nonstick cooking spray.

Next, you are going to want to use cooking scissors and cut the ribs into chunks that are about 3 or 4 ribs in size.

Place the ribs in the Instant Pot and sprinkle them with the paprika.

Place the lid on the Instant Pot and ensure that it is locked into place. Cook on high pressure for 30 minutes.

After the Instant Pot beeps, signaling that the cooking process is done, you will do a quick pressure release and remove the ribs from the Instant Pot, placing them on a baking pan that is lined with foil.

Brush the glaze mixture onto the ribs and place them under the broiler in your oven for a few minutes just to finish them off. Make sure that you do not leave them in the oven for too long because the BBQ sauce contains sugar and it will burn quickly.

3. Instant Pot Ham

Serves 4. Prep Time: 15 Minutes, Cook Time: 30 Minutes

You will need:

One 4-5 pound boneless ham, fully cooked

1 cup of maple syrup

1/2 of a cup of brown sugar

2 tablespoons of Dijon honey mustard

1 teaspoon of allspice

Instructions:

Begin by removing the casing from the ham if there is one. Next, you will score the top of the ham by making cuts diagonally on the top surface about 1 inch apart from each other. This will allow more of the sauce to soak in. Place the ham into the Instant Pot.

In a bowl, you will want to mix the brown sugar, allspice, maple syrup and the honey mustard. Pour this over the top of the ham in the Instant Pot.

Place the lid on the Instant Pot and lock it into place. Cook the ham on high pressure for 30 minutes. After the Instant Pot has completed the cooking process, you are going to do a quick release and remove the ham from the Instant Pot. Slice the ham and serve.

As you can probably already tell, most of these lunch recipes can also be used when you are making dinner as well. You will also find that in the next chapter, there are plenty of dinner recipes that you can switch out and use for lunch recipes.

Of course, what would life be if you could not switch out some of the breakfast recipes for lunch of dinner?

If you are preparing your food to take with you to work, it is a great idea for you to just add a few extra servings to your dinner that you are preparing and simply pack the extra for lunch. These lunch ideas are for those days when you and your family are home or when you are having a get together with family or friends.

Chapter 3- Instant Pot Dinners Five Ingredients or Less

This chapter is going to be broken down into several sections, just like the previous chapters to ensure that you are able to find the recipes that you are looking for all of them using just five ingredients or less. At the end of this chapter, you will find several side dish recipes that you can cook in your Instant Pot as well.

Chicken

1. BBQ Chicken Sandwiches

Serves 4. Prep Time: 15 Minutes, Cook Time: 25 Minutes

You will need:

1.5 pounds of boneless, skinless chicken breasts

8 ounces of your favorite BBQ sauce

Buns for your sandwiches

You can top the chicken with pickles or onions after you make the sandwiches if desired.

Instructions:

Begin by placing the boneless, skinless chicken breasts in the Instant Pot and top with 8 ounces of your favorite BBQ sauce.

Turn your Instant Pot on high pressure and set the timer for 25 minutes. After the chicken has cooked for 25 minutes, you will hear the Instant Pot beep. It is at this time that you can begin toasting your buns if desired.

After the chicken, has cooked for 25 minutes, use the quick pressure release option then you will remove it from the Instant Pot and place it on a plate. Using two forks, you will shred the chicken. Be very careful as it will be hot.

Once the chicken is shredded, place back in the Instant Pot and coat with the leftover BBQ sauce. Place the shredded chicken on the buns, top with onions or pickles if desired and enjoy. You can also add extra BBQ sauce if desired.

2. Salsa Chicken- This chicken can be eaten as a main course as is when it comes out of the instant pot, or it can be shredded and used to make chicken tacos.

Serves 4. Prep Time: 15 Minutes, Cook Time: 20 Minutes

You will need:

> 1 pound of boneless, skinless chicken breast
>
> 1/2 of a teaspoon of salt
>
> 3/4 of a teaspoon of cumin
>
> A pinch of oregano
>
> 1 cup of your favorite salsa
>
> You can also season this with a bit of ground black pepper after it has cooked if desired.

Instructions:

> Begin by mixing the salt, cumin, and oregano in a small bowl then season the boneless skinless chicken breasts with the mixture rubbing the seasonings on both sides of the meat.
>
> After the chicken breasts, have been seasoned, place them in the Instant Pot and cover the chicken with your favorite salsa.
>
> Place the lid on the Instant Pot and lock it into place then choose the poultry option. You will add five minutes to the cooking time, cooking the salsa chicken for 20 minutes in total.

After the Instant Pot beeps, you will use the quick pressure release option and remove the chicken from the Instant Pot, placing it on a plate.

Use two forks to shred the salsa chicken if you are using it for tacos then place it back in the Instant Pot, coating it with the leftover salsa.

Serve hot.

3. Salt Baked Drumsticks- This is a traditional Chinese meal.

Serves 4. Prep Time: 10 Minutes, Cook Time: 50 Minutes

You will need:

> 8 Chicken legs
>
> 1 1/4 tsp. Salt
>
> 1/4 Frontier five spice powder
>
> 2 tsp. Dried Sand ginger
>
> Ground White Pepper to taste- if desired

Instructions:

> Begin by placing the chicken legs in a bowl and sprinkling the dried sand ginger, salt and Frontier five spice powder over them. Toss the chicken with your hands ensuring that they are evenly coated.

> After the chicken legs are evenly coated with the spices, you will place them on a piece of parchment paper and wrap them tightly. It is important that you do not use aluminum foil but only parchment paper. Make sure that you do not stack the chicken legs more than 2 high.

> Place the chicken legs in a shallow dish.

> Next, you will want to place your steamer rack into the Instant Pot and add in 1 cup of tap water. Insert the

dish that you have placed the chicken legs on into the Instant Pot carefully and place it onto the steamer rack.

Lock the lid into place and set on high pressure for about 25 minutes. After the Instant Pot beeps, you will then natural release the pressure for 20 minutes.

After the pressure has been released, remove the lid, opening it away from you and carefully take the dish out of the Instant Pot. Now it is time to unwrap the chicken from the parchment paper.

You can serve this immediately or you can continue cooking it in the oven. If you choose to cook it in the oven, simply pour all of the juice from the dish into a small bowl and place the chicken on a wire rack under the broiler, cooking until the skin browns just a bit. Serve the chicken, using the juice that you placed in the small bowl as a dipping sauce.

4. Fall Off The Bone Whole Chicken- Cooking a whole chicken in the oven can take up to an hour and it can dry the chicken out, however, when you use this recipe and the Instant Pot, you can have a whole chicken cooked in 30 minutes and it is guaranteed to be the best chicken you have ever had.

Serves 4. Prep Time: 10 Minutes, Cook Time: 30 Minutes

You will need:

1 whole chicken

Season All

1/2 of a cup of water

1/2 of a cup of chicken broth

Instructions:

Make sure that you thaw your chicken out before you cook it or it will take much longer to cook. Begin by rubbing the outside of the chicken with the season all. Place your steamer rack in your Instant pot and add in the 1/2 of a cup of water as well as the 1/2 of a cup of chicken broth.

Place your chicken that has been rubbed with season all into the Instant Pot on top of the steamer rack and lock the lid into place. Choose the poultry option then add an extra 15-20 minutes for a 3-4 pound chicken (10 minutes per pound of chicken for total cooking time)

After the Instant Pot beeps, choose the quick steam release option and carefully remove the chicken. Serve hot.

5. Chicken Teriyaki- This can be served on top of white rice or alone.

Serves 4. Prep Time: 15 Minutes, Cook Time: 20 Minutes

You will need:

4 chicken breasts, boneless and skinless

One 21-ounce bottle of teriyaki sauce

1 bag of Oriental vegetable mix, frozen (12 ounces)

2 tsp. cornstarch

3 tsp. Water

Instructions:

Begin by placing the chicken breasts in the instant pot and pour the teriyaki sauce over the chicken. Lock the lid in place and cook for 20 minutes, on the poultry setting.

While the chicken is cooking, you will want to place the mixed vegetables in a bowl that is microwave safe then place them in the microwave for 1 minute at a time until they are thawed. Drain the vegetables.

Mix the cornstarch and 3 teaspoons of water together in a small bowl.

After the Instant Pot beeps, you will do a quick steam release, then remove the chicken from the Instant pot, shred using two forks and place back into the Instant Pot.

Choose the sauté setting and mix in the cornstarch and water as well as the vegetables mix well sautéing just until everything is heated evenly. About 2 minutes.

Serve over white rice if desired.

6.Basil Chicken and Tomato Pasta

Serves 4. Prep Time: 10 Minutes, Cook Time: 5 Minutes

You will need:

One 1 pound package of Rotini pasta

1 pounds of boneless skinless chicken breasts, cooked

2 Roma tomatoes

2 teaspoons of pesto

1/2 of a pound mozzarella cheese

Instructions:

Begin by placing the pasta in the Instant pot with enough water to cover it. Lock the lid in place and cook on high pressure for about 5 minutes.

While the pasta is cooking, you will chop the tomato, cooked chicken breast and cut the mozzarellas into small cubes. Once you are done with this, your pasta should be done.

Release the steam, using the quick release option and then drain the water from your pasta. Place the pasta back into the Instant Pot, (just to keep it warm) add in the chicken, pesto, tomatoes and mozzarella cheese. Mix well. The Instant Pot should still be warm enough to melt the cheese, however, if it is not, you can turn it to the sauté option for a few minutes. Serve warm.

7.Chicken Tacos- You will serve this on 8 flour tortillas

Serves 4. Prep Time: 10 Minutes, Cook Time: 20 Minutes

You will need:

2 boneless skinless chicken breasts

2 14.5 ounce cans of diced tomatoes with chilies

1 teaspoon of salt

2 ounces of Mexican blend cheese

2 teaspoons of sour cream

Instructions:

Begin by placing the chicken breasts in the Instant Pot and sprinkle with chicken. Cover the chicken breasts with the 2 cans of diced tomatoes with chilies. Lock the lid in place and then choose the poultry option cooking for 20 minutes.

After the Instant Pot has beeped, choose the quick release option and then remove the lid. Take the chicken out of the Instant Pot and place it on a plate. Shred it using two forks.

Serve the chicken in a warm tortilla shell with a bit of sour cream on top. You could also choose to add lettuce to the tacos.

8.Caesar Chicken

Serves 4. Prep Time: 15 Minutes, Cook Time: 30 Minutes

You will need:

4 chicken breasts, boneless and skinless, thawed

One 12 ounce bottle of Caesar dressing

1/2 of a cup of parmesan cheese, shredded

Instructions:

Begin by placing the chicken breasts in the Instant Pot. Cover the chicken with the Caesar dressing. Place the lid on the Instant Pot and lock it into place. Cook on the poultry setting for 20 minutes.

After the Instant Pot has beeped indicating that the cooking process is done, use the quick release option and open the lid. Serve the chicken with Caesar salad.

9. BBQ Bacon Chicken

Serves 4. Prep Time: 15 Minutes, Cook Time: 20 Minutes

You will need:

4 chicken breasts, boneless, skinless and thawed

One 18 ounce bottle of your favorite BBQ sauce

3/4 of a teaspoon of hickory liquid smoke

1 package of bacon cooked crispy and then chopped into small pieces

Instructions:

Begin by placing the chicken in the Instant Pot. In a separate bowl, you will mix the BBQ sauce, the liquid smoke, and the bacon. After mixing up the BBQ sauce mixture, pour it over the chicken.

Close the lid and ensure that it is locked into place. Using the poultry setting cook the chicken for 20 minutes.

After the Instant Pot beeps indicating that the cooking process is complete, use the quick release option and serve the chicken hot.

10.Instant Pot Queso Chicken

Serves 4. Prep Time: 15 Minutes, Cook Time: 20 Minutes

You will need:

4 chicken breasts, boneless, skinless and thawed

3/4 of a cup of Salsa Con Queso

1 10 ounce can of Rotel tomatoes, drained

1 4 ounce can of green chilies, drained

1/2 of a teaspoon of garlic salt

Instructions:

Begin by placing the chicken in the Instant Pot. Top the chicken with the salsa con queso, then sprinkle the garlic salt over the salsa con queso. Next, you will add in the Rotel tomatoes and finally top it off with the green chilies.

Close the lid on the Instant Pot and ensure that it is locked into place. Using the poultry setting, you will cook this for 20 minutes. After the Instant Pot beeps, indicating that the cooking process is complete, you will use the quick release option.

Serve the chicken hot. This is great with rice.

11. French Onion Chicken

Serves 4. Prep Time: 15 Minutes, Cook Time: 20 Minutes

You will need:

4 chicken breasts, boneless, skinless and thawed

1 10.5 ounce can of condensed French onion soup

1/2 of a cup of sour cream

Instructions:

Begin by placing the chicken in the Instant Pot. In a separate bowl, you will mix the condensed French onion soup and the sour cream. Pour the soup mixture over the chicken and close the Instant Pot lid.

Ensure that the lid is locked into place and then cook using the poultry setting for 20 minutes. After the Instant Pot beeps, indicating that the cooking process is complete, do a quick release and open the Instant Pot.

Serve the chicken hot.

12.Olive Garden Chicken

Serves 4. Prep Time: 15 Minutes, Cook Time: 20 Minutes

You will need:

4 chicken breasts, boneless, skinless and thawed

1 16 ounce jar of Olive Garden brand, Italian dressing

1/4 of a cup of parmesan cheese, grated

Instructions:

Begin by placing the chicken in the instant pot. In a separate bowl, you will then mix the Italian dressing and the parmesan cheese. Pour the dressing mixture over the chicken and close the lid to the Instant Pot.

Ensure that the lid is locked into place and then using the poultry setting, you would cook the chicken for 20 minutes.

After the Instant Pot beeps, indicating that the chicken is done cooking, you will do a quick release and serve the chicken hot.

13.Greek Chicken

Serves 4. Prep Time: 10 Minutes, Cook Time: 20 Minutes

You will need:

4 chicken breasts, boneless and skinless, thawed

One 16 ounce bottle of Ken's brand Steak House Greek dressing with feta cheese, black olives and imported olive oil

Kalamata olives, pitted and sliced

1/4 of a cup of Feta cheese

Instructions:

Begin by placing the chicken in the Instant Pot. Pour the salad dressing over the top of the chicken and close the lid to the Instant Pot. Make sure that the lid is locked into place and cook the chicken using the poultry setting for 20 minutes.

After the Instant Pot beeps, indicating that the cooking process is complete, you will do a quick release and remove the chicken from the Instant Pot. Top the chicken with the sliced Kalamata olives and the feta cheese.

Serve hot.

14.Salsa Chicken with a Twist

Serves 4. Prep Time: 10 Minutes, Cook Time: 20 Minutes

You will need:

4 chicken breasts, boneless, skinless and thawed

1 16 ounce jar of your favorite salsa

1 8 ounce package of cream cheese, softened

1 cup of sharp cheddar cheese, shredded

Optional- 1 can of black beans drained and rinsed or 1 can of corn, drained

Instructions:

Begin by placing the chicken in the Instant Pot. In a separate bowl, you are going to mix the salsa, cream cheese, and optional ingredients if you are using any.

Pour the salsa mixture over the chicken in the Instant Pot and close the lid.
Ensure that the lid is locked into place and cook using the poultry setting for 20 minutes.

After the Instant Pot beeps, indicating that the chicken is done cooking, you will want to do a quick release and sprinkle the cheddar cheese over the chicken. The cheese should melt quickly. Serve hot. Leftovers are great to use for making tacos and burritos.

15.Orange, Cranberry Chicken

Serves 4. Prep Time: 15 Minutes, Cook Time: 20 Minutes

You will need:

4 chicken breasts, boneless, skinless and thawed

1 cup of Catalina dressing

1 14 ounce can of cranberry sauce with whole berries

1 packet of onion soup mix

1 tablespoon of orange marmalade

Instructions:

Begin by placing the chicken in the Instant Pot. In a separate bowl, you will mix the dressing, onion soup mix, cranberry sauce and the marmalade, stirring to ensure that it is mixed well.

Pour this mixture over the chicken and place the lid on the Instant Pot. Ensure that the lid is locked into place and then using the poultry setting, cook the chicken for 20 minutes.

After the Instant Pot beeps, indicating that the cooking process is complete, you will do a quick pressure release and serve the chicken hot. This is great with rice.

16. Tortellini- While this is not a chicken recipe, I wanted to include it in the book because it is so easy to make.

Serves 4. Prep Time: 5 Minutes, Cook Time: 10 Minutes

You will need:

One 20 ounce package of cheese tortellini

One 24 ounce jar of your favorite pasta sauce

4 cups of mozzarella, shredded

1/2 of a teaspoon of garlic powder

2 teaspoons of basil

Instructions:

Begin by spraying the inside of your Instant Pot with nonstick cooking spray to ensure that the cheese does not stick to the sides.

Pour 1/2 of the pasta sauce or 12 ounces into the bottom of the Instant Pot. Take 1/2 of the tortellini and create an even layer in the sauce. Sprinkle the garlic powder over the tortellini then sprinkle 2 cups of shredded mozzarella cheese on top of it.

Next, you will add the rest of the pasta sauce, another layer of tortellini and the last 2 cups of mozzarella cheese. Finally, sprinkle with basil.

Close the Instant Pot and ensure that the lid is locked into place. Cook on high pressure for 10 minutes.

After the Instant Pot beeps indicating that the pasta is done cooking, do a quick pressure release and serve the tortellini hot.

17. Honey Mustard Chicken

Serves 4. Prep Time: 10 Minutes, Cook Time: 20 Minutes

You will need:

4 chicken breasts, boneless, skinless and thawed

One 12 ounce bottle of Dijon mustard

1/3 of a cup of honey

Instructions:

Begin by placing the chicken in the Instant Pot. In a separate bowl, you will want to mix the honey and the Dijon mustard together. Pour the mustard mixture over the chicken and place the lid on the Instant Pot.

Lock the lid into place and cook, using the poultry setting for 20 minutes. After the Instant Pot beeps, indicating that the chicken is completely cooked, you are going to do a quick pressure release and serve the chicken hot.

18. Sweet and Sour Chicken

Serves 4. Prep Time: 10 Minutes, Cook Time: 20 Minutes

You will need:

4 chicken breasts, boneless, skinless and thawed

One 12 ounce bottle of sweet and sour sauce

One 20 ounce can of pineapple chunks

1 white onion, chopped

2 bell peppers, green, chopped

Instructions:

Begin by placing the chicken breasts in the Instant Pot and then cover with the juice from the pineapple chunks. In a separate bowl, you will place the pineapple chunks, the sweet and sour sauce, the onions and peppers and mix them well.

Pour the mixture over the top of the chicken in the Instant Pot and place the lid on the Instant Pot. Ensure that the lid is locked into place and then using the poultry setting cook for 20 minutes.

After the Instant Pot beeps indicating that the cooking process is complete, you will want to do a quick pressure release and serve the chicken hot, over rice.

19.Creamy Ranch Chicken

Serves 4. Prep Time: 15 Minutes, Cook Time: 20 Minutes

You will need:

4 chicken breasts, boneless and skinless, thawed

Two 10.75 ounce cans of cream of chicken with herb soup

1 packet of ranch dressing mix

Instructions:

Begin by placing the chicken in the Instant Pot. In a separate bowl, you will mix the two cans of cream of chicken soup with the ranch dressing mix. Pour the soup mixture over the chicken and place the lid on top of the Instant Pot.

Ensure that the lid is locked into place and then using the poultry setting cook for 20 minutes.

After the Instant Pot beeps, you will want to do a quick pressure release and serve the chicken hot. This is great served with pasta.

20.Hickory and Brown Sugar BBQ Chicken

Serves 4. Prep Time: 15 Minutes, Cook Time: 30 Minutes

You will need:

4 chicken breasts, boneless and skinless, thawed

One 18 ounce bottle of your favorite BBQ sauce

1/2 of a cup of brown sugar

Instructions:

Begin by placing the chicken in the bottom of the Instant Pot. In a separate bowl, you will mix the BBQ sauce and the brown sugar. Pour the BBQ sauce mixture over the chicken and place the lid on the Instant Pot.

Make sure that the lid is locked into place and then cook the chicken by choosing the poultry setting. After the Instant Pot beeps, indicating that the chicken is done cooking, you will want to do a quick pressure release and remove the chicken from the Instant Pot setting it on a cutting board.

Shred the chicken using two forks and then place it back into the Instant Pot, mixing it well to ensure that it is completely coated with the BBQ sauce mixture.

Serve on buns.

21. Honey Sesame Chicken

Serves 4. Prep Time: 15 Minutes, Cook Time: 20 Minutes

You will need:

4 chicken breasts, boneless, skinless and thawed

8 ounces of Asian toasted sesame dressing

3/4 of a cup of honey

Sesame seeds

Green onions, chopped

Instructions:

Begin by placing the chicken in the Instant Pot. Next, you will mix the dressing and the honey in a separate bowl. Pour this mixture over the chicken. Place the Instant Pot lid in place and ensure that it is locked.

Using the poultry setting, you will cook the chicken for 20 minutes. After the Instant Pot beeps, indicating that the chicken is done cooking, you will do a quick pressure release and remove the chicken from the Instant Pot.

Sprinkle the sesame seeds and the chopped green onions over the chicken and serve with rice.

22. Peach Salsa Chicken

Serves 4. Prep Time: 15 Minutes, Cook Time: 20 Minutes

You will need:

4 chicken breasts, boneless, skinless and thawed

One 18 ounce jar of peach preserves

One 16 ounce jar of chunky salsa

Instructions:

Begin by placing the chicken in the bottom of the Instant Pot. In a separate bowl, you will mix the salsa and the peach preserves together ensuring that it is mixed well.

Pour the salsa mixture over the chicken and place the lid on the Instant Pot. Ensure that the lid is locked into place and then choose the poultry setting, cooking the chicken for 20 minutes.

After the Instant Pot beeps, indicating that the chicken is done cooking, you will use the quick pressure release option and serve the chicken hot.

23. Cheesy Broccoli Chicken

Serves 4. Prep Time: 15 Minutes, Cook Time: 20 Minutes

You will need:

4 chicken breasts, boneless, skinless and thawed

One 10.75 ounce can of condensed broccoli cheese soup

1/2 of a cup of sour cream

1 cup of shredded sharp cheddar cheese

One 10 ounce package of frozen broccoli florets

Instructions:

Begin by placing the chicken in the Instant Pot. In a separate bowl, you will want to mix the broccoli cheese soup, cheddar cheese, and sour cream. Stir well to ensure that it is evenly mixed.

Pour the soup mixture over the chicken and place the lid on the Instant Pot. Ensure that the lid is locked into place and using the poultry setting cook the chicken for 20 minutes.

After the Instant Pot beeps signaling that the cooking process is complete, you will use the quick pressure release option and then serve the chicken hot. This is great with a side of rice.

24. Hawaiian BBQ Chicken

Serves 4. Prep Time: 15 Minutes, Cook Time: 20 Minutes

You will need:

4 chicken breasts, boneless, skinless and thawed

1 18 ounce bottle of your favorite BBQ

1 20 ounce can of pineapple chunks

Directions:

Begin by pouring ½ of a cup of the pineapple juice from the pineapple chunks into the Instant Pot. Next, you are going to place the chicken into the Instant Pot, in the pineapple juice.

Drain the rest of the pineapple juice out of the can of pineapple chunks, discarding the juice and setting the chunks to the side.

In a bowl, you will mix the BBQ sauce and the pineapple chunks, stirring well to ensure that it is completely mixed.

Pour the BBQ sauce mixture over the chicken in the Instant Pot and then place the lid on the Instant Pot.

Check to ensure that the lid is locked into place and cook the chicken using the poultry setting for 20 minutes. After the Instant Pot beeps, you will want to do a quick pressure release and serve the chicken hot. This can also be shredded and made for Hawaiian BBQ chicken sandwiches.

25.Creamy Mushroom Chicken

Serves 4. Prep Time: 15 Minutes, Cook Time: 20 Minutes

You will need:

4 chicken breasts, boneless, skinless and thawed

2 cans of cream of mushroom soup

2 7 ounce cans of mushroom stems and pieces, drained

1 packet of onion soup mix

1/2 of a cup of French's onions

Instructions:

The first thing that you want to do is to place the chicken in the bottom of the Instant Pot. After you have placed the chicken in the bottom of the Instant Pot, you are going to want to mix the mushroom stems and pieces, the mushroom soup, the onions soup mix and the French's onions in a bowl.

Make sure that it is mixed well and then pour over the chicken that is in the Instant Pot. Next, you are going to place the lid on the Instant Pot and ensure that it is locked into place.

Cook the chicken using the poultry setting for 20 minutes. After the Instant Pot beeps, indicating that the chicken is done cooking, you will want to do a quick pressure release and serve the chicken hot. This is great served over rice.

26. Chicken Stroganoff

Serves 4. Prep Time: 10 Minutes, Cook Time: 30 Minutes

You will need:

4 chicken breasts, boneless and skinless

1 can of cream of mushroom soup, about 10 ounces

8 ounces of cream cheese

16 ounces of sour cream

1 package of egg noodles

Instructions:

Begin by placing the chicken breasts in the instant pot and topping with the cream of mushroom soup. Chop the cream cheese into cubes and toss on top of the mushroom soup. Lock the lid into place and cook for 30 minutes on the poultry setting.

While the chicken is cooking in the Instant Pot, follow the directions on your package of egg noodles and cook them on the stovetop. Drain after cooking.

After the Instant Pot has beeped, do a quick release and remove the chicken from the Instant Pot, placing it on a plate and shredding it. After the chicken has been shredded, toss it back into the instant pot and add in 12 ounces of your sour cream. Mix well. Add the noodles into the mixture and stir until it is mixed thoroughly. Serve topped with a bit of sour cream.

27. Hawaiian Pineapple Chicken

Serves 4. Prep Time: 15 Minutes, Cook Time: 20 Minutes

You will need:

> 1 pound of boneless skinless chicken breasts that have been cut into chunks
>
> 1 pineapple, chopped into chunks after it has been skinned and the core has been removed
>
> 2 tbsp. of light brown sugar
>
> 2 tbsp. of soy sauce

Instructions:

Place all of the ingredients into the Instant Pot and lock the lid into place. Cook using the poultry setting for 20 minutes. Do a quick pressure release.

This is a great dish to serve with rice and/or broccoli.

Pork & Fish

1.Pot Carnitas

Serves 4. Prep Time: 15 Minutes, Cook Time: 90 Minutes

You will need:

2 pounds of pork shoulder, boneless and cut into chunks about 2 inches in size

1 tbsp. Taco seasoning

3/4 teaspoon of salt

The juice from 2 oranges

The juice from 1 lime

1 tbsp. Ghee

Instructions:

Begin by placing the pork into the Instant pot. Sprinkle with the Taco seasoning, salt and a bit of black pepper if desired. Toss to ensure all of the pork is coated well.

Place the juice from the oranges and the lime into a measuring cup and then fill up to the 1 cup line with water. Pour the mixture over the pork in the Instant Pot.

Lock the lid in place and press the manual setting. Set the time to 50 minutes. After the pork has cooked, choose the cancel option to allow for natural release.

After the steam has released, remove the lid from the Instant Pot and choose the saute option. Carefully, using two forks begin to shred the pork. Let this cook until there is almost no liquid left in the pot, making sure that you are stirring occasionally to ensure that the meat does not stick or burn. This is going to take about 25 more minutes.

When you get to the point that there is almost no liquid left in the Instant Pot, you will mix in the Ghee and continue cooking until the pork has just begun to brown. This will take about five more minutes.

Serve hot. This is great with rice, and avocado.

2. Broccoli, Ham and Cheese Potatoes

Serves 2. Prep Time: 10 Minutes, Cook Time: 15 Minutes

You will need:

4 baking potatoes

Diced ham

Your favorite cheese

Broccoli

Butter

Instructions:

Begin by washing the potatoes and placing them in the Instant Pot for 15 minutes on high pressure. After the potatoes have baked for 15 minutes, you will use the quick release option to release the steam, remove the potatoes from the Instant Pot, splitting each of them open.

Fill each potato with broccoli and ham. Place back into the Instant Pot and cook on high pressure for an additional three minutes.

After the potatoes have finished cooking, use the quick release option to release the pressure and then take them out of the Instant Pot. Sprinkle with cheese before serving.

3. Simple Pulled Pork

Serves 4. Prep Time: 15 Minutes, Cook Time: 75 Minutes

You will need:

1 Pork Shoulder

1 cup chicken broth

1/2 of an onion, sliced

1 garlic clove, minced

1 cup of your favorite BBQ sauce

Instructions:

Begin by placing the 1 cup of chicken broth into the Instant Pot. Next, you will want to cut the pork shoulder into pieces that are about 3 to 4 inches in size.

You can at this point season the pork with salt and pepper if you wish. Place the cut up pork into the Instant Pot with the chicken broth. Sprinkle the minced garlic on top of the pork and top with the sliced onions.

Lock the lid into place on the Instant Pot and then using the manual setting, set the timer for 60 minutes.

After the Instant Pot beeps, use the quick release option and then you will take the pork out of the Instant Pot and shred it with two forks. If the meat does not shred easily, place it back in the Instant Pot and continue to cook for an additional 15 minutes, using the manual setting.

Once the pork is shredded, you can add the cup of BBQ sauce to it as well as whatever liquid is left in the bottom of the Instant Pot. Toss to coat well and serve on buns.

4. Pork Tenderloin Roast and Beans

Serves 6. Prep Time: 15 Minutes, Cook Time: 60 Minutes

You will need:

2 cans of black beans, rinsed and drained

1 jar of your favorite salsa

1 can of diced tomatoes

1 pork tenderloin roast

1 onion, chopped finely

You may also choose to season this with salt, pepper, or garlic

Instructions:

If you are choosing to use salt and pepper, you can begin by rubbing the salt and pepper on the outside of the roast. If you want to season it with garlic, you can insert small bits of garlic into the roast.

Begin by choosing the sauté option on the Instant Pot and brown the roast either in cooking spray or you can use a tablespoon of olive oil if you have it on hand.

After the roast has been browned on all sides, place the beans, diced tomatoes, salsa and onion into the Instant Pot.

Using the manual setting set the timer to 60 minutes.

After the Instant Pot beeps, signaling that it is done, you will want to allow the steam to release naturally before serving the roast and beans.

5. Roasted Pork Loin

Serves 4. Prep Time: 15 Minutes, Cook Time: 60 Minutes

You will need:

1.5 pounds of pork loin

3 cups of chicken stock

1 large onion

4 cloves of garlic

2 Tbsp. of cornstarch mixed with ½ of a cup of water

Salt and pepper if desired

Instructions:

If you are seasoning the pork loin with salt and pepper you will want to do this first, then place it into the Instant Pot. If you are not using salt and pepper, simply place the pork loin into the Instant Pot.

Pour the three cups of chicken stock onto of the pork loin. Slice the onion and toss it on top of the pork loin. Next, you will want to crush the garlic or mince it and toss it on top of the onions.

Lock the lid into place and cook for 60 minutes using the manual setting. Once the pork is done cooking you will want to allow the pressure to release naturally.

After the pressure has released, you will then add in the cornstarch and water mixture stirring well and switch over to the sauté mode bringing everything up to a boil. Serve hot.

This is great served with mashed potatoes. You can also add vegetables into this recipe such as carrot, mushrooms or any vegetable of your choice.

6. Mushroom Pork Chops

Serves 5. Prep Time: 15 Minutes, Cook Time: 30 Minutes

You will need:

About 10 pork chops or as many as you would like to cook

1 can of cream of mushroom soup

1/2 of a cup of ketchup

Instructions:

Begin by placing the pork chops in the Instant Pot. Next, you will place the cream of mushroom soup in a bowl and mix it with the 1/2 of a cup of ketchup.

Pour this mixture over the pork. Lock the lid into place and cook on high pressure for 30 minutes. Allow the steam to naturally release and serve with your favorite side dishes.

7. Salmon, Broccoli, and potatoes

Serves 2. Prep Time: 5 Minutes, Cook Time: 4 Minutes

You will need:

1 salmon fillet

2 cups broccoli

3 cups new potatoes of choice

Salt and pepper to taste 1 tablespoon butter

Herbs for seasoning

Instructions:

Chop the florets and set it aside and Put water at the bottom of IP

Season the potatoes with salt, pepper, and herbs, doing the same with the salmon and broccoli

Put the potatoes on a steaming rack and then with some butter. Set it to steam for about two minutes, and flick the valve to instantly release it

Put the florets and the salmon on a rack and do the same for another 2 minutes.

Once done, let it cool down so it's warmed, serving it immediately.

8. Spicy lemon Salmon

Serves 4. Prep Time: 5 Minutes, Cook Time: 4 -7 Minutes

You will need:

4 stock eye salmon fillets, about an inch thick

2 tablespoons chili pepper

Pepper to taste

2 lemons, one for juicing the other for slicing

Salt to taste

1 cup water

Instructions:

Season the salmon with pieces, and then put the steam rack on the bottom with handles up. Place the salmon on there in a single layer.

Put leftover seasoning on top, and then a cup of water to the pot, avoiding the seasoning on the salmon.

Cover and then press manual and then cook either for 4-7 minutes, depending on salmon sizes. For thicker pieces, move towards seven and for smaller, you should have it around four.

When done, let it naturally release to the pressure needed. You can serve it instantly.

9. Instant pot Alaskan Cod

Serves 1. Prep Time: 5 Minutes, Cook Time: 5 – 9 Minutes

You will need:

1 fillet of Alaskan cod

Salt and pepper for seasoning

A cup of cherry tomatoes

2 Tablespoons butter

Instructions:

In a glass dish (Oven Safe) that fits IP, put the tomatoes in there, and then cut the fillet and put it on top. Season it to taste.

Put 2 parts butter on top of each, and then drizzle with olive oil.

Put a cup of water into the pot and then the trivet. Put the dish in trivet and lock lid.

Put it on high for about 9 minutes if unthawed, 5 if thawed.

Naturally release pressure and then serve it.

<u>Beef</u>

1. Taco Stuffed Peppers

Serves 4. Prep Time: 10 Minutes, Cook Time: 10 Minutes

You will need:

1/2 of a pound of ground beef

1 taco seasoning pack

4 green bell peppers

Lettuce

Cheese

Tomatoes are optional

Instructions:

Begin by removing the seeds from your green bell peppers, only cutting the top of them off to create a bowl. Place the peppers on a steamer rack in the Instant Pot with about 1/2 of a cup of water. Lock the lid in place and cook on high for about 5 minutes. Use the quick pressure release, remove the peppers and set them to the side to cool.

After the peppers are cooked, you will want to crumble up the ground beef into the Instant Pot and using the sauté setting you will brown the beef. Once the beef begins to brown, drain it. Add 1/4 of a cup of water and the taco seasoning to the ground beef and allow to sauté until it thickens.

While the beef is sautéing, you will check your bell peppers to ensure that they have cooled and make sure that there is no water in the bottom of them. If there is water, simply dump it out. During this time you will also chop your lettuce and tomatoes if you are using them.

After the beef is done sautéing, you will scoop it into the peppers and top with a bit of cheese. Place the peppers back into the Instant Pot, lock the lid in place and cook for an additional 5 minutes. Use the quick release option, remove the peppers from the Instant Pot and top with lettuce. Serve.

These are also great topped with tomatoes and sour cream.

2. Chili Beans Beef

Serves 4. Prep Time: 10 Minutes, Cook Time: 15 Minutes

You will need:

1 pound of ground beef

1 can of diced tomatoes with green chilies

2 cans of dark red kidney beans, rinsed and drained

1/2 of an onion diced

Chili seasoning

Instructions:

Begin by turning your Instant Pot on the sauté mode. Break up your ground beef into the Instant Pot, add in the diced onion and cook it until the beef is brown. After the beef has browned, you will mix in the chili seasoning, 2 cans of beans, and diced tomatoes.

At this point, you will have to decide how thick you want your chili to be. If you want it to be thinner, simply add a cup or two of water to the Instant Pot.

Close the lid and lock it into place. Cook on high pressure for 15 minutes and when it is done, use the quick release option.

This is great served topped with cheese or on top of rice.

3. Beef Soup with Mixed Vegetables

Serves 4. Prep Time: 15 Minutes, Cook Time: 20 Minutes

You will need:

1 pound of ground beef

1 bag of frozen stew or soup vegetables (celery, carrots, potatoes, onions and green beans)

48 ounces of chicken broth

2 cans of diced tomatoes

1 teaspoon of garlic, minced

Instructions:

Begin by setting the Instant Pot on the sauté mode and crumble up the ground beef in it. Add in the minced garlic and sauté until the meat is no longer pink. Next, you will add in all of the other ingredients and turn off the sauté mode.

Once all of the ingredients have been added, you will turn on the soup mode, lock the lid into place and cook for 20 minutes. When it is done, you will do a quick release and serve hot.

This is great served with parmesan cheese.

4. Enchilada Dip

Serves 4. Prep Time: 15 Minutes, Cook Time: 5 Minutes

You will need:

1.5 pounds of ground beef

1 can of chili beans

1 can of red enchilada sauce, about 10 ounces

2 cups of shredded cheddar cheese

Chips

Instructions:

Using the sauté setting on your Instant Pot, you will sauté the ground beef until it is brown and then drain off any extra fat.

After the beef is browned, place it into a small baking dish that will fit into the Instant Pot stir the chili beans into the dish with the beef, as well as the enchilada sauce and 1 cup of the cheddar cheese mixing well. Sprinkle remaining cheese on top. Place the baking dish down into the instant pot.

Lock the lid in place and cook on high pressure for 5 minutes. Use the quick release option and then remove the dish from the Instant Pot. Serve hot with tortilla chips

5. Mushroom Beef Stew

Serves 4. Prep Time: 15 Minutes, Cook Time: 20 Minutes

You will need:

2 packages of frozen stew vegetables

1.5 pounds of beef stew meat

1 can of cream of mushroom soup

1 can of tomato soup, condensed

1 package of onion soup mix

Instructions:

Begin by placing the stew meat into the Instant Pot and using the sauté mode, brown the beef stew meat on all sides. While this is browning, mix the mushroom soup, tomato soup and the onion soup mix in a bowl.

After the meat has browned, turn off the sauté mode. Add in the frozen vegetables and then pour the soup mixture over everything.

Lock the lid into place and cook on high for 20 minutes. When the stew is done cooking, you will use the quick release and serve it hot.

6.Swedish Meatballs

Serves 4. Prep Time: 10 Minutes, Cook Time: 4 Minutes

You will need:

1 pound of frozen meatballs

¼ of a cup of butter

1/3 of a cup of flour

3 cups of beef broth

1 cup sour cream

Salt and pepper are optional

Instructions:

The night before you are going to cook the meatballs, set them in the refrigerator so they can thaw. When you are ready to make the meatballs, you will set your Instant Pot to the simmer mode and place the butter in the Instant Pot.

Allow the butter to melt and then gradually begin whisking the flour in with the butter so that it looks a bit crumbly. Next, you will begin to slowly add in your beef broth, whisking it along with the flour-butter mixture so that it does not clump. This is going to take about 4 minutes to do.

After the beef broth has been mixed and begins to look a bit like gravy, you will add in the cup of sour cream as well as salt and pepper if desired.

Once all of this is done, you will place the meatballs into the mixture, close the lid and lock it into place. Cook the meatballs on manual for 3 minutes and serve hot.

7. Cabbage Rolls

Serves 4. Prep Time: 15 Minutes, Cook Time: 20 Minutes

You will need:

A head of cabbage

A cup of rice

1/4 of an onion diced

1 pound of ground beef (you can season this with Italian seasoning if desired)

A can of diced tomatoes

Instructions:

The first thing that you are going to want to do is cook your rice. You can use your Instant Pot to do this if you want to, using 2 cups of water per 1 cup of rice that you are cooking.

While the rice is cooking you will want to blanch your cabbage leaves. In order to do this, you will want to cut the bottom off of the head of cabbage and carefully peel the leaves off. Place the leaves in boiling water for about 2 minutes.

Remove them from the water and place in a strainer or on a paper towel to dry. While you are cooking the rice and blanching the cabbage leaves you will want to brown the ground beef and onions on the stove. By the time you are done doing this, the rice will be cooked.

After the rice has cooked and the beef is browned, you will mix the two together in a bowl. Scoop this mixture into the cabbage leaves and roll them up. After you have rolled all of the cabbage rolls, you will place them on the steam rack in your Instant Pot and steam them for 5 minutes.

While the cabbage rolls are steaming, you will heat up the can of diced tomatoes.

After the cabbage rolls are steamed, you will do a quick steam release and serve them topped with the diced tomatoes.

Sides

What is a dinner without side dishes to go along with it? Not only is the Instant Pot going to be able to help you prepare your main dishes in record time but it is also going to help you make all of your side dishes as well!

1. Mushrooms and Asparagus Crowns

Serves 4. Prep Time: 5 Minutes, Cook Time: 4 Minutes

You will need:

1 pound of Asparagus Crowns

¼ of a cup of chicken broth

½ of a cup of mushrooms, fresh

Salt and pepper to taste

Instructions:

The first thing that you will want to do is to wash your vegetables. Make sure that you wash the mushrooms well because they are often covered in soil. Next, you will want to cut the asparagus into 2-inch pieces.

Place all of the ingredients into the Instant Pot and stir well making sure that everything is mixed well. Place the lid on the Instant Pot and cook on low pressure for 4 minutes. After the Instant Pot beeps, signaling that the asparagus crowns and mushrooms are done cooking, you will use the quick release option and remove the lid. Serve hot.

This is a great side dish to serve with salmon.

2. Balsamic Mushrooms

Serves 4. Prep Time: 5 Minutes, Cook Time: 5 Minutes

You will need:

1/3 of a cup of EVOO (extra virgin olive oil)

3 cloves of garlic, minced

1 pound of mushrooms, fresh and sliced

3 tablespoons of balsamic vinegar

Salt and pepper to taste

Instructions:

Begin by pouring the 1/3 of a cup of EVOO into the Instant Pot and choosing the saute option.

Next, you will add in the minced garlic as well as the sliced fresh mushrooms, coating them in the EVOO.

Sauté the mushrooms and minced garlic for about 3 minutes, or until they begin to soften. Once the mushrooms have softened.

Pour the balsamic vinegar over the mushrooms and stir gently to coat. Allow this to cook for about 2 more minutes. Serve hot and season with salt and pepper.

3. Green Beans

Serves 4. Prep Time: 5 Minutes, Cook Time: 3 - 5 Minutes

You will need:

1 pound of green beans, fresh

1/4 of a cup of bacon bits

1/2 of a teaspoon of butter

Salt and pepper to taste

Instructions:

Begin by snapping off the ends of the green beans then wash them. After the green beans are prepped for cooking, you will place a cup of water in the bottom of the Instant Pot and then place the steamer into the pot.

Place the bacon and the green beans into the Instant Pot, lock the lid in place and cook on high pressure for 3 minutes. If you like very soft green beans, cook for up to 5 minutes. Use the quick pressure release and then remove the green beans and bacon from the Instant Pot, placing them in a bowl.

After the green beans are in a bowl you will mix in the butter, which will melt very quickly.

Serve hot.

4. Buttery Mashed Potatoes

Serves 4. Prep Time: 5 Minutes, Cook Time: 9 - 15 Minutes

You will need:

2 pounds of potatoes, white potatoes work best

2 teaspoons of butter

4 teaspoons of milk

1 cup of water

Salt and pepper to taste

Instructions:

Begin by placing the 1 cup of water into the Instant Pot. Cut your potatoes in half and place them inside the water in the Instant Pot. Choose the manual setting and cook for 9 minutes.

After the potatoes have cooked for 9 minutes, use the quick release method and check to see if they are soft. If the potatoes are not soft, cook on manual for an additional 5 minutes.

After the potatoes have cooked, place them in a bowl with the milk, butter, salt, and pepper. Mash the potatoes and serve hot.

5. Easy Honey Glazed Carrots

Serves 4. Prep Time: 10 Minutes, Cook Time: 5 Minutes

You will need:

1 pound of baby carrots

1 teaspoon of honey

2 teaspoons of butter

1/3 of a cup of brown sugar

1/2 of a cup of water

*you can also throw in a pinch of parsley if you want to give them some color. Salt and pepper are also optional.

Instructions:

Wash your carrots and place them in the Instant Pot. In a small bowl, you will then mix the butter, brown sugar and the honey.

Add the 1/2 of a cup of water to the Instant Pot and top everything with the honey mixture. Lock the lid into place and choosing the manual setting, you will cook the carrots for 5 minutes. After the carrots have cooked, use the quick release option, sprinkle with parsley, salt or pepper if desired and serve hot.

6. Roasted Red Potatoes

Serves 4. Prep Time: 10 Minutes, Cook Time: 8 Minutes

You will need:

4 tablespoons of butter

2 pounds of baby red potatoes

2 sprigs of rosemary

4 garlic cloves

1/3 of a cup of vegetable stock

Salt and pepper if desired

Instructions:

You will begin by placing the butter into the Instant Pot and choosing the sauté setting. After the Instant Pot has heated up and the butter begins to melt, you will add in the rosemary sprigs, garlic cloves, and the potatoes.

Mix everything up until the potatoes are completely coated in the butter mixture. Leave the Instant Pot on the sauté setting and continue stirring the potatoes gently as they cook for about 8 minutes. You will want to poke the potatoes to ensure that each of them is cooked through.

Next, you will add in the vegetable stock, lock the lid into place and cook on high pressure for 8 minutes.

After the potatoes have cooked, you will want to do a natural release. After the pressure has released, remove the potatoes from the Instant Pot and use salt and pepper if desired to season them. Serve hot.

Conclusion

The Instant Pot really is the all in one appliance that every busy person needs in their kitchen. The Instant Pot will not only allow you to cook all of these amazing recipes that you have found in this book in no time at all but it is also going to allow you to clear up some of that counter space, doing the work of 7 appliances all in one small appliance.

Because the Instant Pot is so easy to use and because it saves so much time, it not only is great for those that are very busy but it is a great way to ensure that you and your family are eating home cooked meals every night.

Right now, it seems that people are becoming more and more aware of the foods that they are eating and are wanting to eat more home cooked meals and the Instant Pot ensures that you can do this.

Now, thanks to the Instant Pot, instead of ordering pizza or hitting the local drive thru, you can prepare a healthy homemade meal in no time flat. **On top of that, you can create these meals using this book with only five ingredients or less.**

Who could have ever imagined that creating healthy delicious meals with only five ingredients or less was possible? And who would have imagined that most of them would only take 20 minutes or less to cook?

I hope that you have enjoyed the recipes in this book and that you have found some that you will be adding to your regular meal plan.

43473938R00072

Made in the USA
Middletown, DE
10 May 2017